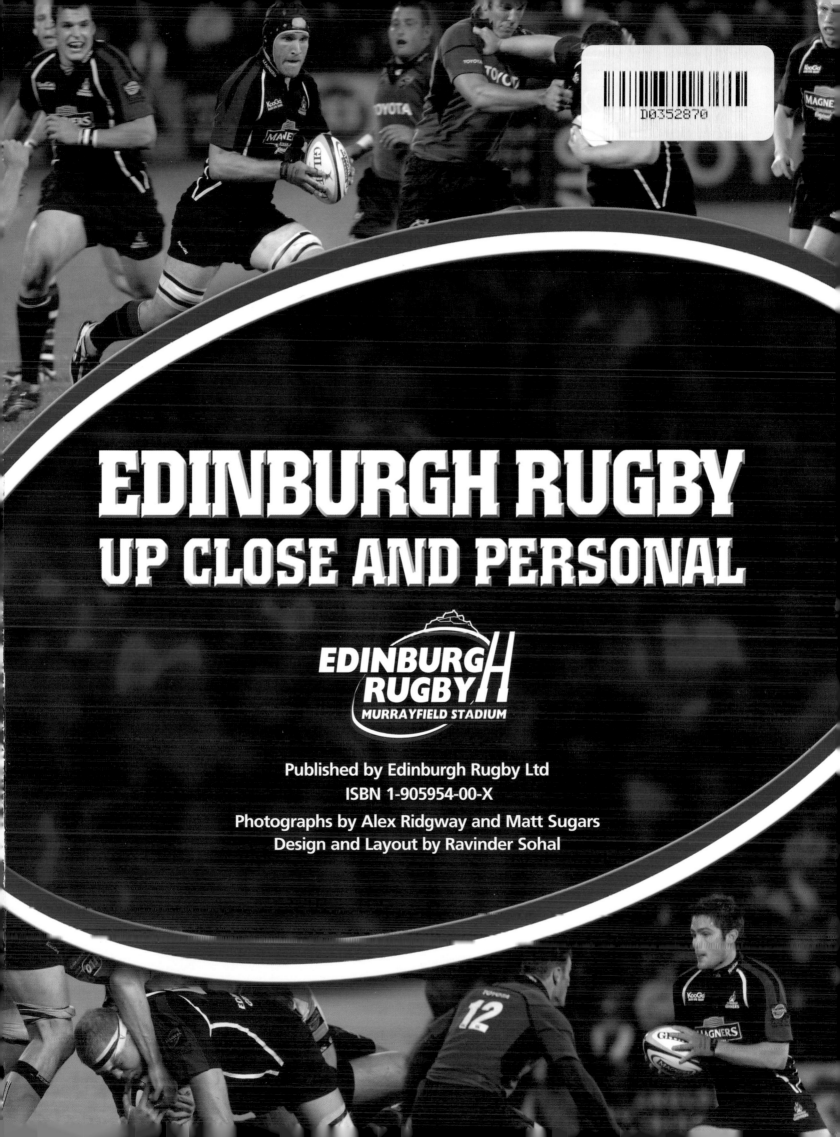

EDINBURGH RUGBY
UP CLOSE AND PERSONAL

EDINBURGH RUGBY
MURRAYFIELD STADIUM

Published by Edinburgh Rugby Ltd
ISBN 1-905954-00-X

Photographs by Alex Ridgway and Matt Sugars
Design and Layout by Ravinder Sohal

A foreword from the boardroom

Early in 2006, the name Gunners disappeared from official usage at the club and the team reverted to its original name; Edinburgh Rugby. This change was yet another development in Season 2006/7, a momentous year for pro-rugby in Scotland. The SRU has taken the lead in attempting to bring outside investors into the professional game and we in turn are committed to working in association with the Union over the long term to bring success to Scottish rugby at the pro-team level.

As part of that process the new owners of Edinburgh Rugby have committed themselves to a five year business plan covering the first phase of development which, depending on the fortunes of the team, and the willingness of the Edinburgh public to support the team, could easily require a further £3m and possibly as much as £5m to be invested in Edinburgh Rugby.

These are the hard facts of Scottish professional rugby in its current form, and while everyone aspires to imitate the success of Sale or Munster, the investors in the team have their eyes firmly open to the fact that they may never see their investment again. Without success on the field and a surge in enthusiasm from the public only an optimist would expect to see a financial return, but if you are reading this you already know that rugby is not about money anyway.

Many of you out there have asked for some kind of statement of intent from the owners of the club. Now that we have a few games under our collective belts it's time to start painting something of a vision for where we hope to go. We do of course intend to be unashamedly commercial in our approach to Edinburgh Rugby and we very much hope to build a vibrant financially healthy pro-rugby team in Edinburgh. But that's not the end game.

What we desperately want is to bring success to Edinburgh. It is essential for the good health of rugby football in Scotland that the game is successful at International level, at Club level and also at Pro-team level. It's here that we hope to make our contribution. With a relatively small playing base no one is expecting world domination, but over the next five years it is our stated intention to bring one major championship back to Murrayfield.

We intend to deliver that success using as many Scottish internationalists as possible. Our supporters want to see a team packed with internationalists and we want to see our most promising players picked for Scotland. Naturally we intend to continue to be the pre-eminent team in Scotland and we aim to continue to supply the lion's share of the Scotland team. It's important that talented younger players see Edinburgh as the logical stepping-stone to a Scotland place. We hope to give the players the security and continuity of a long-term commitment and in return we expect total dedication and commitment to the club. Under no circumstances will we permit the club to be seen as a feeder to the Guinness Premiership; we hope to begin the process of encouraging great Scottish players to come back and play their professional rugby in Scotland.

The down side of fielding so many capped players is that we will, of course, lose key members of the squad to international duty at key stages of the Magners League. Our opponents suffer from the same problem, but we have given ourselves an additional mission to maintain the depth of the squad in anticipation of losing key personnel at key times in the league. This is actually much harder than it sounds. Besides the obvious matter of fitting any given player's availability to the gaps in the squad and the budget, there are also very strict criteria surrounding the number of non-European players who are entitled to be named in our 22 for a Magners League squad (two!) and a further raft of immigration rules at the Home Office which make it difficult to employ non-capped players. Nonetheless you can rest assured that with Lynn Howells now in place we will continue to scour the planet for the best talent around who can maintain the challenge during the internationals and world cup, but who themselves won't be subject to international call ups. This year we got lucky with Matt Mustchin... if we could just find another five!

Aside from the business aspects of Edinburgh Rugby we hope to be able to enjoy the whole

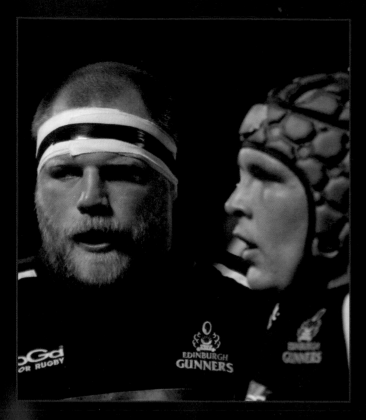

experience of being involved in a sport which we believe enriches the lives of so many people in so many ways. As rugby people, we understand that rugby is about taking part in a wonderful game, it's about great friendships forged around the globe, it's about a well-earned beer after a hard fought match. For the players it's a life long learning experience, which teaches everything you need to know about control, psychology, group dynamics with a smattering of physics, logic and maths thrown in. Once you add referees into the equation, you can also begin to glimpse the capriciousness and sheer incomprehensibility of the decision making process!

For spectators, rugby is about coming into an environment which is passionate and knowledgeable but which is welcoming and safe. We hope to continue to develop that tradition and to enjoy the journey along the way.

The mere fact that you are playing or watching rugby dispenses with those awkward introductions. The simple fact that you are here reading this means you are a welcome part of the global rugby family. Like it or not, you are now part of the world's most fun free-masonry which extends from Lerwick to Capetown, and you don't even have to buy an apron! When rugby people meet, the introductory formalities have already been dispensed with. Try visiting Connacht, Ulster,

Llanelli or any of the other Magners League and Heineken Cup grounds you'll soon find that the crowds there are just friends you haven't met yet.

Away from Murrayfield we'd hope to nurture and support a tradition of supporters travelling in numbers and we will obviously be linking up with the supporters club to work out how we do that. It's great to be a part of the rugby community especially when so much in sport dwells on the negative. A visit to Landsdowne Road will confirm that even the middle of the opposition rugby crowd is still a welcoming, fun place to be and the players do respond to the support. Where a football crowd takes pride in unveiling a tawdry banner saying "welcome to hell" it's satisfying to note that the rugby equivalent still just reads "welcome". We hope to play a big part in continuing that worthy tradition at Murrayfield.

That's not to say the warm welcome will ever extend to the points on offer. Our stated aim is to turn our home turf into Fortress Murrayfield and to start a trend of bringing home points from every away match. It is a great credit to the Scottish Rugby Union that we were able to inherit such a great squad of players. Chris Paterson is an inspirational captain and has a great rugby brain. It was Chris who identified the simple strategy for success in the Magners League. All you have to do is win your home games and make sure of at least a bonus point away - and you'll win the League. Chris and his team have already begun to deliver that vision with a hard fought bonus point at Ospreys and a draw away from home to Connacht so far this season, not to mention three magnificent back to back wins at home against Leinster, Ulster and Glasgow and, of course, the famous victory away to Munster, which brought Edinburgh their first ever success at Thomond Park.

We hope you enjoy this photographic record of the early part of the 2006/2007 season as captured by club photographers Matt Sugars and Alex Ridgway. Injuries and selection policy mean that we can't bring you a profile on every player in the squad, but there will certainly be more opportunities in future.

Rest assured we will keep up the hard work of telling other people what to do...

The Directors

CHRIS PATERSON

EDINBURGH RUGBY
MURRAYFIELD STADIUM

Chris Paterson is the captain of Edinburgh Rugby. As well as providing inspirational leadership to the team, Chris is also one of the most exciting and creative wings in world rugby. Chris was instrumental in the famous victory over Munster at Thomond Park, the first ever win at that stadium by Edinburgh.

Friday 25th August 2006

Sale V Edinburgh

Pre-season Friendly

Sale 30 Edinburgh 14

10

SCOTT MURRAY

Scott Murray is currently playing some of the best rugby in his long and distinguished career. Scott is the automatic first choice at lock for Scotland, and of course, for Edinburgh Rugby. By 2007 there is every possibility that Scott may well become Scotland's most capped player and deservedly so.

16

18

19

HUGO SOUTHWELL

Hugo Southwell is a big favourite with the fans at Edinburgh Rugby. Hugo is Scotland's first choice full back and is exciting in attack and equally solid in defence as can be seen from this powerful big hit leading to turn over ball against Munster.

23

26

SIMON WEBSTER

Simon is a unique character, the eternal optimist for whom the metaphorical glass is always totally full. Simon is without doubt one of the great wings in world rugby and his unpredictable running has become the hallmark of his game for both Edinburgh and Scotland.

More action from Ospreys V Edinburgh

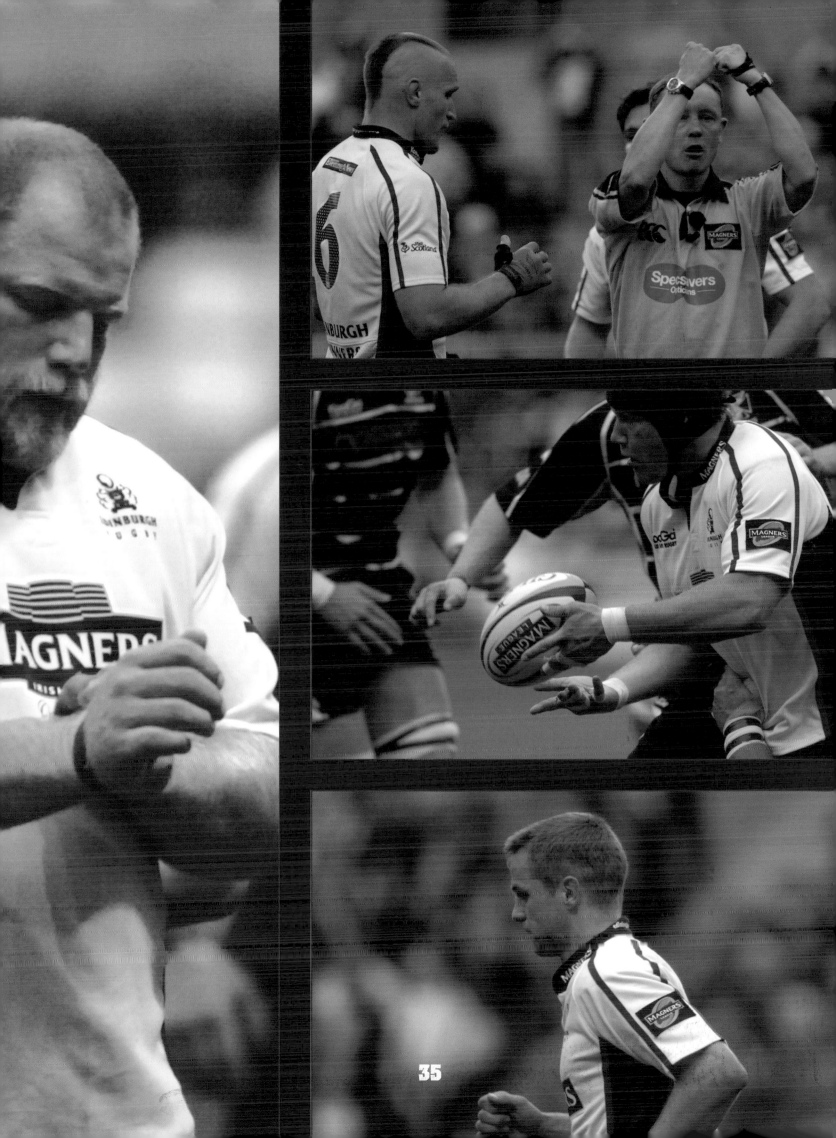

ALLAN JACOBSEN

Allan Jacobsen of Scotland and Edinburgh is one of the greatest prop forwards in the modern game. Allan is also surprisingly nimble in the loose and has turned his ball carrying skills to Edinburgh's advantage a number of times this season.

MARCUS DI ROLLO

Marcus has become a regular fixture in the Scotland team and is also first choice at centre for Edinburgh. A strong feature of Marcus' game is his rock solid defence coupled with electrifying pace, which can be turned on at a moments notice.

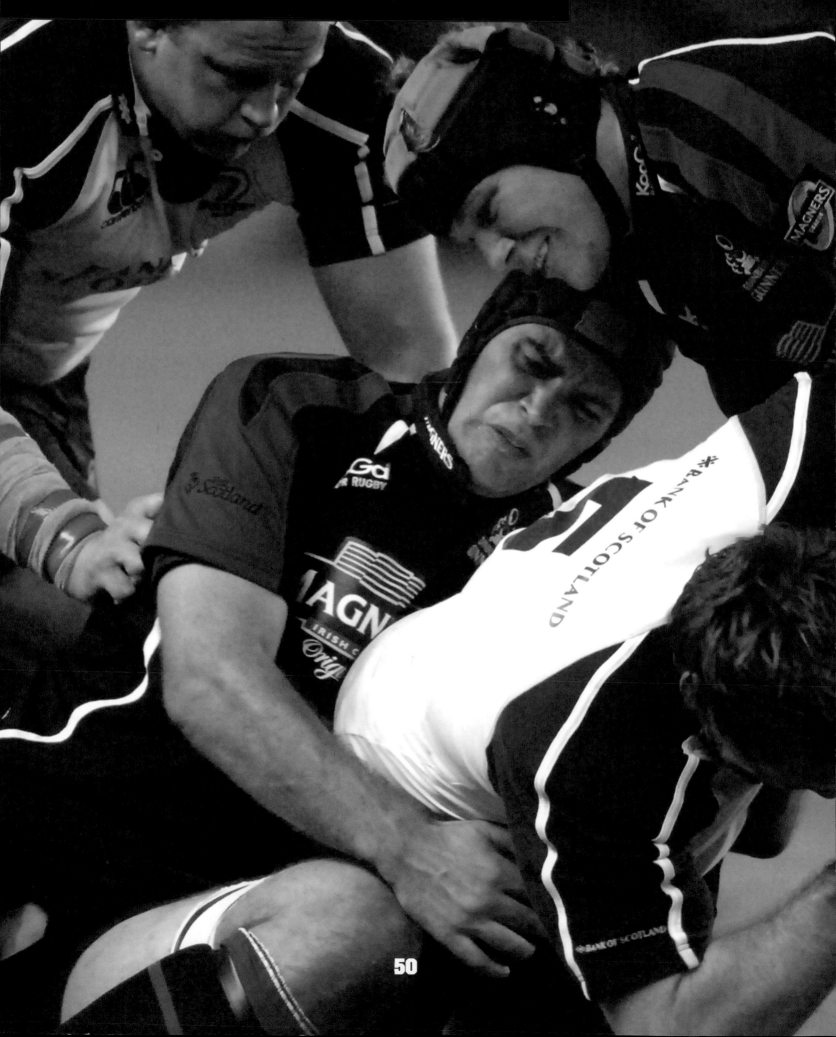

50

51

BEN CAIRNS

Ben has broken through to grab a well-merited place in a number of games for Edinburgh this season. One of the highlights of Ben's early season was his match-winning try against Ulster. Ben is a Scotland Under 21 Cap and has represented Scotland in the IRB World Sevens.

Friday 15th September 2006
Edinburgh V Ulster
Magners League
Edinburgh 20 Ulster 15

MICHAEL BLAIR

EDINBURGH RUGBY
MURRAYFIELD STADIUM

Mike Blair is now well established as Scotland's first choice scrum half. Mike is justifiably famous for his superb service at scrum and line out as well as his darting runs and rock solid defence. Mike is tipped to command a central position in World Rugby for years to come.

More action from Edinburgh V Ulster

PHIL GODMAN

Phil Godman has made the number 10 shirt his own this season. His running with the ball in hand has proved to be a major weapon in Edinburgh's armoury and Phil is also a place kicker of distinction. One of the highlights of the season to date from Phil was the sensational chip through the Agen defence, which resulted in a try for Hugo Southwell and Mike Pyke.

70

DOUGIE HALL

Dougie Hall is Scotland's first choice hooker and naturally commands the number 2 shirt at Edinburgh Rugby. Dougie is uncompromising in the scrum and equally at home in the loose where he is constantly looking to carry the ball at every available opportunity.

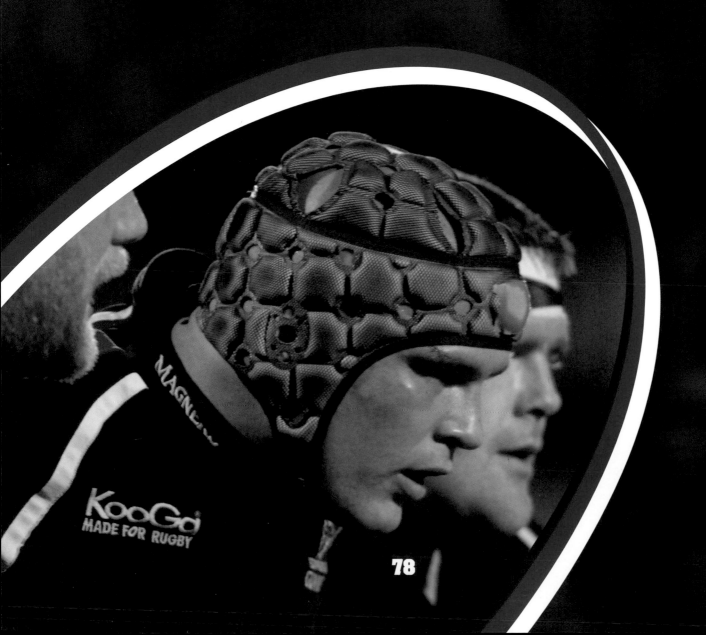

KooGa
MADE FOR RUGBY

More action from Edinburgh V Connacht

ROSS RENNIE

Ross is a fast developing talent who has played some huge games for Edinburgh this season which has resulted in the youngster being fast tracked into Frank Hadden's Scotland squad for the match against Romania. Ross is definitely one to watch for the future.

Friday 29th September 2006
Edinburgh V Glasgow Warriors
Magners League
Edinburgh 14 Glasgow Warriors 9

MATT MUSTCHIN

Equally at home in the back row or in the second row Matt has become the automatic choice to partner Scott Murray. Matt has been at his best this season in the loose with a great appetite for carrying the ball to Edinburgh's advantage, most notably in the victory over Munster where Matt had an outstanding match in a season of outstanding matches.

More action from Edinburgh V Glasgow Warriors

ROB DEWEY

Rob has broken through this season to become a firm fixture in the centre for Edinburgh. The chief hallmark of his game is his ability to cross the gain line time and time again. Rob's size and strength play a major role in his highly physical approach to the game, both in attack and defence.

ALASDAIR STROKOSCH

EDINBURGH RUGBY
MURRAYFIELD STADIUM

Alasdair has a Scots mother and German father but his heart is 100% Edinburgh. The Mohawk hair cut and relentlessly positive approach to the game are the two factors which mark Alasdair out from the crowd. His fearsome tackling and superb vision in the loose are just two notable aspects of his constantly developing game.

DAVE DULEY

Dave has been a great servant to Edinburgh Rugby bringing welcome injection of experience to the pack. Dave is particularly effective at clearing out the opposition from rucks. The best evidence of this was seen in Dave's commanding performance against Glasgow.

122

ALASDAIR DICKINSON

This has been a big season for Alasdair who has broken through the ranks and is now a regular contender for the number 3 jersey. Alasdair is very strong in the scrum and is equally at home in the loose where his strong running has proved a major part of Edinburgh's attacking flair. Alasdair scored a try in the momentous victory over Munster at Thomond Park.

CRAIG SMITH

Craig Smith is the leading choice for Scotland's number three jersey. Rock solid scrumaging and a massive presence in the loose are two of the stand out aspects of Craig's game. Craig missed a number of matches with a calf injury but has made a very welcome return to the first team.

25

EXIT
SORTIE ◀ll

THE SUPPORTERS

Of course, none of this would have been possible without the support and enthusiasm of the growing army of Edinburgh Rugby enthusiasts. We salute you.

THE TEAM COACHES

Henry Edwards did a sterling job in filling in as head coach during the early part of the season and was instrumental in putting together a new coaching team featuring Rob Moffat who looks after the backs and Ian Paxton who is responsible for the forwards. Lynn Howells took over the team in September and has gone from strength to strength in pursuit of the first major honours for Edinburgh Rugby.